FINGERPICKING
IRISH SONGS

ISBN 978-1-61780-725-1

HAL•LEONARD®
CORPORATION
7777 W. BLUEMOUND RD. P.O. BOX 13819 MILWAUKEE, WI 53213

In Australia Contact:
Hal Leonard Australia Pty. Ltd.
4 Lentara Court
Cheltenham, Victoria, 3192 Australia
Email: ausadmin@halleonard.com.au

Visit Hal Leonard Online at
www.halleonard.com

Dicey Reilly

Traditional Irish Folk Song

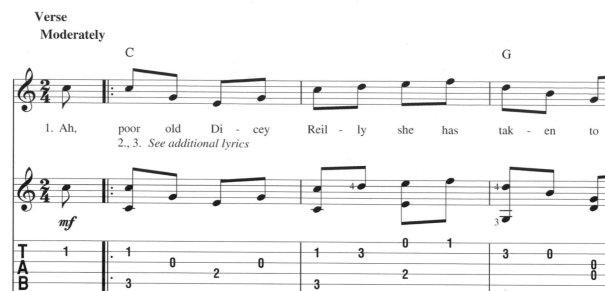

1. Ah, poor old Di-cey Reil-ly she has tak-en to the
2., 3. *See additional lyrics*

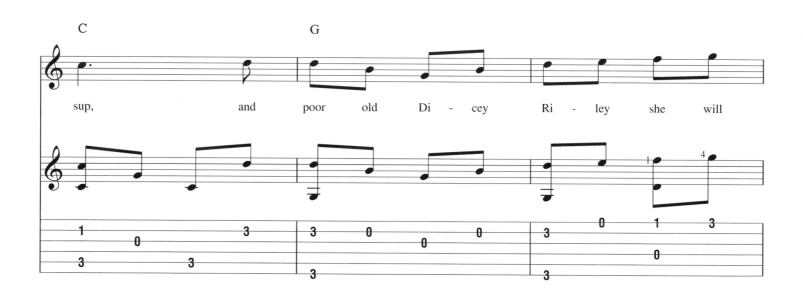

sup, and poor old Di-cey Ri-ley she will

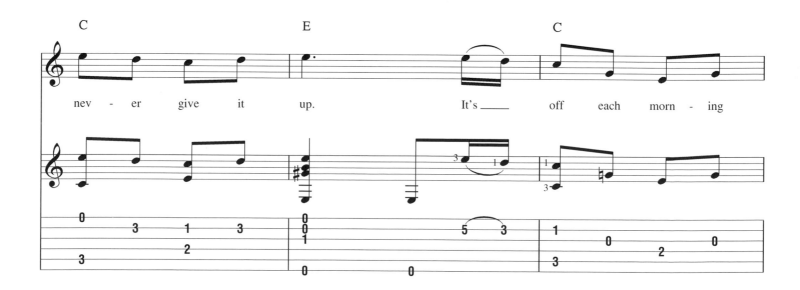

nev-er give it up. It's ___ off each morn-ing

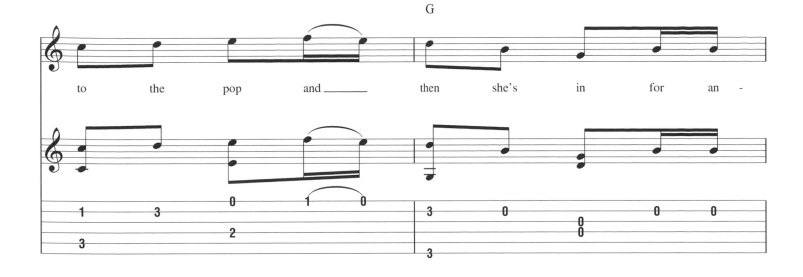

to the pop and _____ then she's in for an -

oth - er lit - tle drop. Ah, the heart of the rowl is Di - cey

Reil - ly. 2. She ley.

Additional Lyrics

2. She walks along Fitzgibbon Street with an independent air;
   And then it's down to Summerhill, at her the people stare.
   She says, "It's nearly half past one and it's time I had another little one."
   Ah, the heart of the rowl is Dicey Reilly.

3. She owns a little sweet shop at the corner of the street,
   And ev'ry evening after school I go to wash her feet.
   She leaves me there to mind the shop, while she nips in for another little drop.
   Ah, the heart of the rowl is Dicey Reilly.

Down by the Salley Gardens

Traditional Irish Folk Song

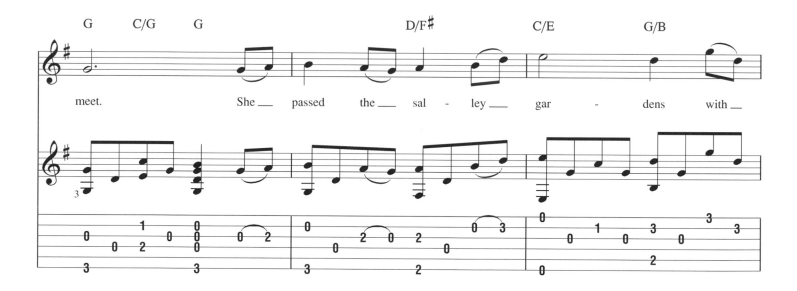

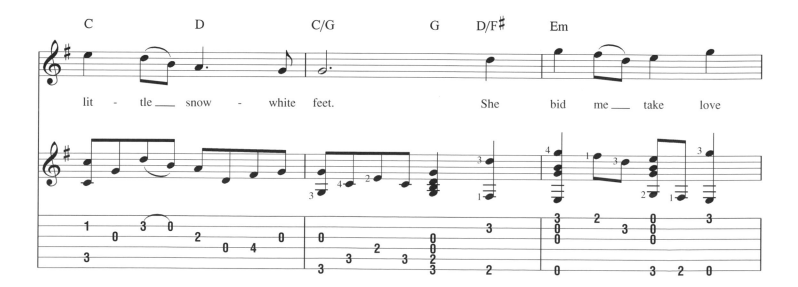

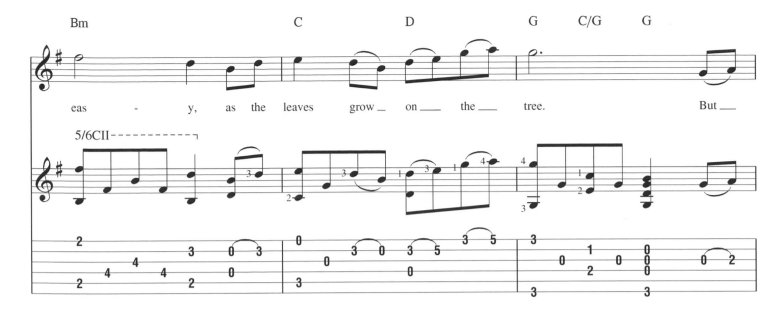

eas - y, as the leaves grow on the tree. But

I, be-ing young and fool - ish, with her did not a-

gree.   2. In a tears.

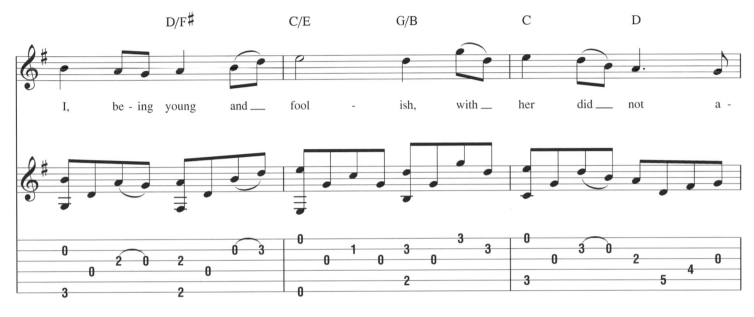

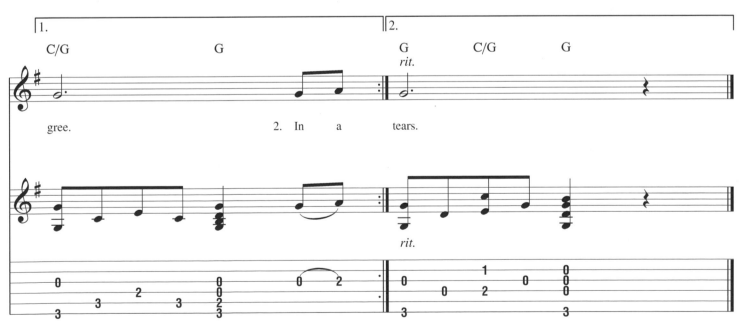

Additional Lyrics

2. In a field down by the river, my love and I did stand.
   And leaning on my shoulder, she laid her snow-white hand.
   She bid me take life easy, as the grass grows on the weirs.
   But I was young and foolish, and now am full of tears.

The Foggy Dew

Traditional Irish Folk Song

Verse
Moderately

1. O - ver the hills I _____ went one
2. *See additional lyrics*

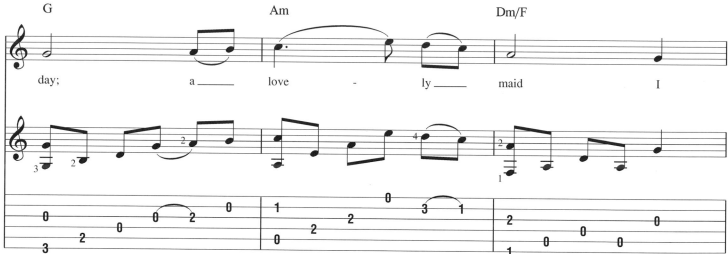

day; a _____ love - ly _____ maid I

spied. _____ With her coal black _____

hair   and her man - tle so green,   an ____

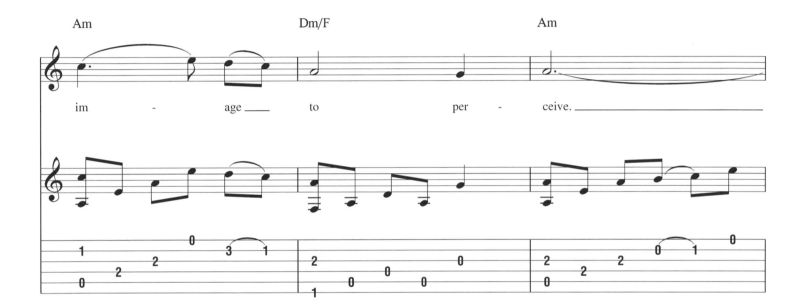

im - age ____ to per - ceive. _____

____   Says I,   "Dear girl,   will you

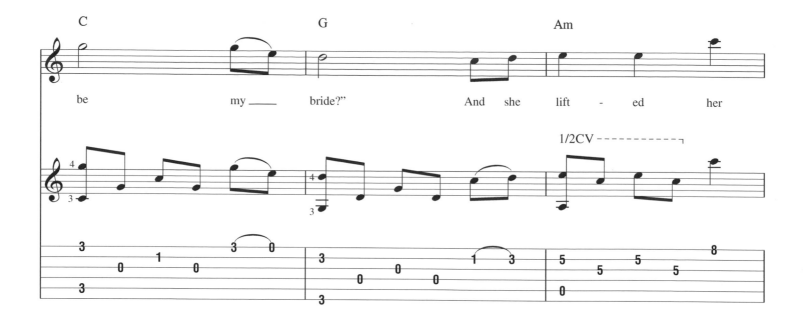

be my bride?" And she lift - ed her

eyes of blue. She

smiled and said, "Young man, I'm to

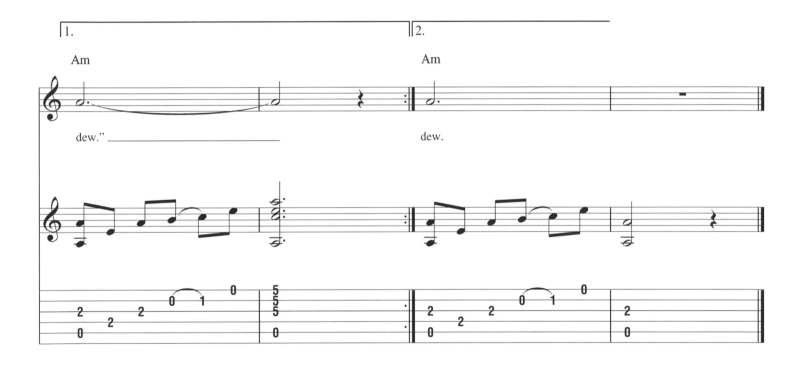

Additional Lyrics

2. Over the hills I went one morn;
   A-singing I did go.
   Met this lovely maid with her coal black hair,
   And she answered soft and low.
   Said she, "Young man, I'll be your bride,
   If I know that you'll be true."
   Oh, in my arms, all of her charms
   Were casted in the foggy dew.

The Galway Piper

Irish Folk Song

Drop D tuning:
(low to high) D-A-D-G-B-E

Intro
Lively

Verse

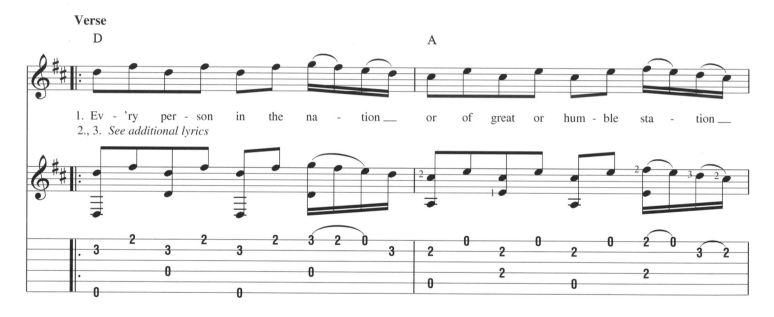

1. Ev - 'ry per - son in the na - tion — or of great or hum - ble sta - tion —
2., 3. *See additional lyrics*

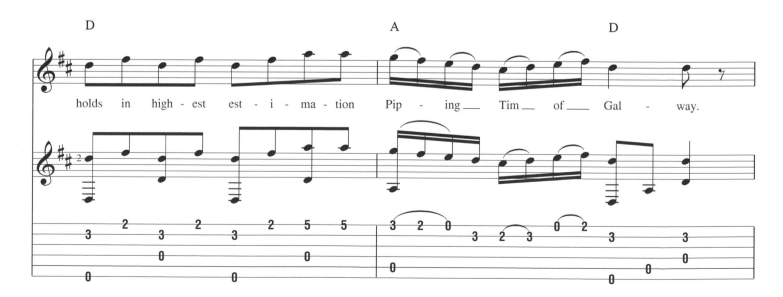

holds in high - est est - i - ma - tion Pip - ing — Tim — of — Gal - way.

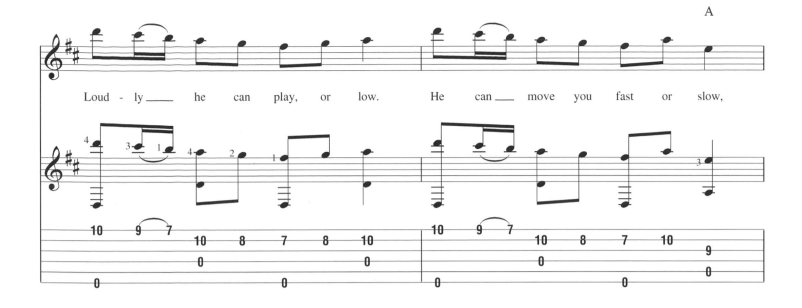

Loud - ly ___ he can play, or low. He can ___ move you fast or slow,

touch your ___ hearts or stir your toe, Pip - ing ___ Tim of Gal - way.

Additional Lyrics

2. When the wedding bells are ringing,
His the breath to lead the singing.
Then in jigs the folks go swinging;
What a splendid piper!
He will blow from eve to morn;
Counting sleep a thing of scorn.
Old is he, but not outworn.
Know you such a piper?

3. When he walks the highways pealing,
'Round his head the birds come wheeling.
Piping Tim of Galway.
Thrush and linnet, finch and lark
To each other twitter, "Hark!"
Soon they sing from light to dark
Pipings learnt in Galway.

I'll Tell Me Ma

Traditional Irish Folk Song

Verse
Moderately

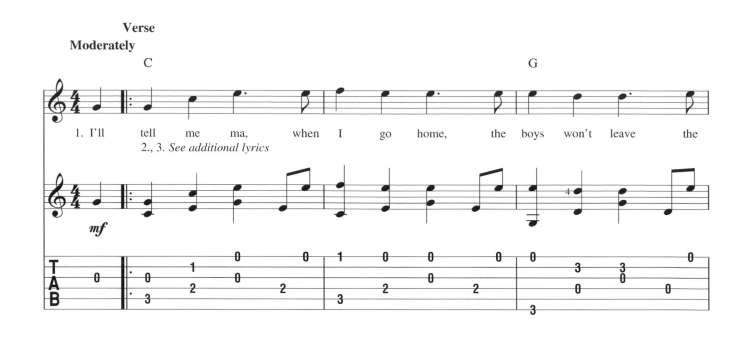

1. I'll tell me ma, when I go home, the boys won't leave the
2., 3. *See additional lyrics*

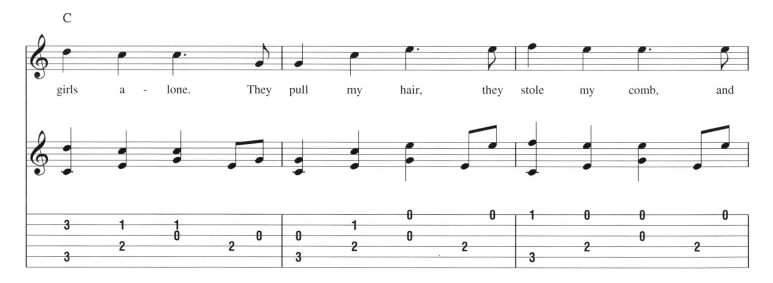

girls a - lone. They pull my hair, they stole my comb, and

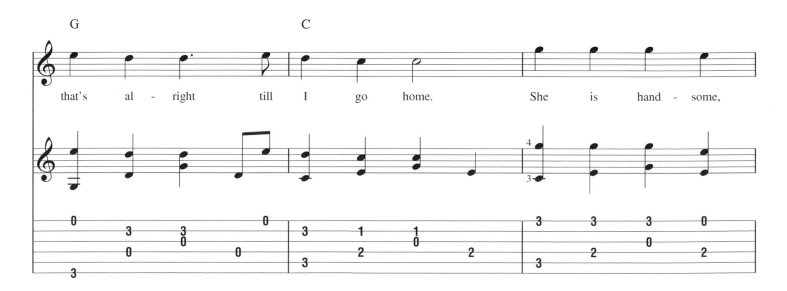

that's al - right till I go home. She is hand - some,

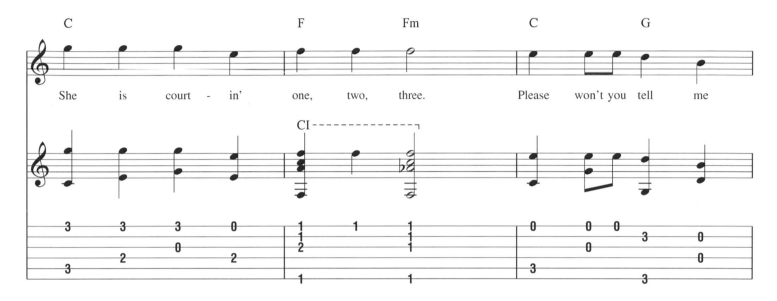

Additional Lyrics

2. Now, Albert Mooney says he loves her;
   All the boys are fightin' for her.
   They rap the door and ring the bell,
   Saying, "Oh, my true love, are you well?"
   Out she comes, as white as snow,
   Rings on her fingers, bells on her toes.
   Old Jenny Murphy says she'll die,
   If she doesn't get the fellow with the roving eye.

3. Let the wind and the rain and the hail blow high
   And the snow come shov'lin' from the sky.
   She's as nice as apple pie,
   And she'll get her own lad by and by.
   When she gets a lad of her own,
   She won't tell her ma when she gets home.
   Let them all come as they will,
   But it's Albert Mooney she loves still.

The Gypsy Rover

Traditional Ballad

Chorus

dy.   Ah,   dee,   do,   ah, dee, do, dah, day.

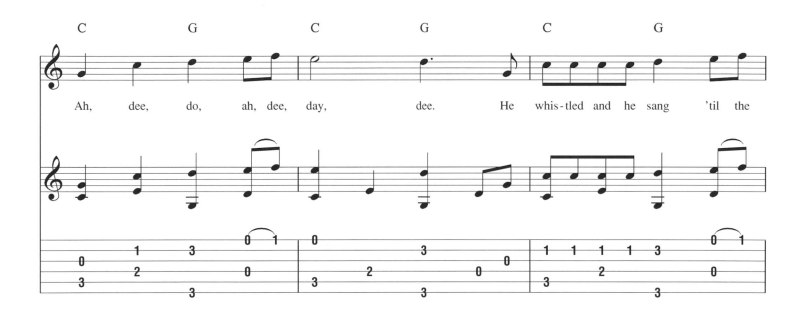

Ah, dee, do, ah, dee, day,   dee.   He whis-tled and he sang 'til the

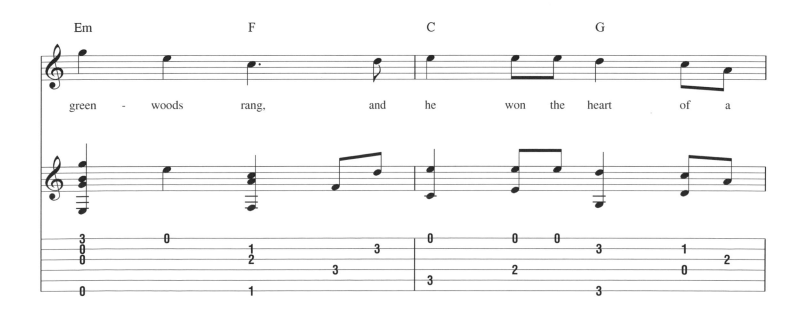

green - woods rang,   and he   won the heart   of a

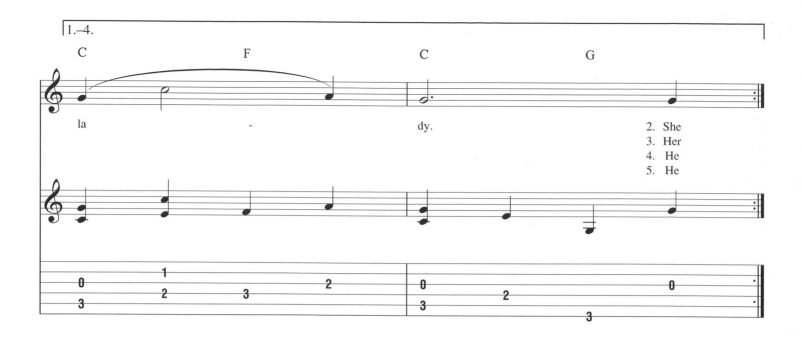

la - dy.

2. She
3. Her
4. He
5. He

la - dy.

Additional Lyrics

2. She left her father's castle gate;
   She left her own fine lover.
   She left her servants and her state
   To follow her gypsy rover.

3. Her father saddled up his fastest steed
   And roamed the valley all over.
   Sought his daughter at great speed,
   And the whistlin' gypsy rover.

4. He came at last to a mansion fine
   Down by the river Claydee.
   And there was music and there was wine
   For the gypsy and his lady.

5. "He is no gypsy, my father," she cried,
   "But lord of these lands all over.
   And I shall stay 'til my dying day
   With my whistlin' gypsy rover."

Londonderry Air

Traditional Irish

Drop D tuning:
(low to high) D-A-D-G-B-E

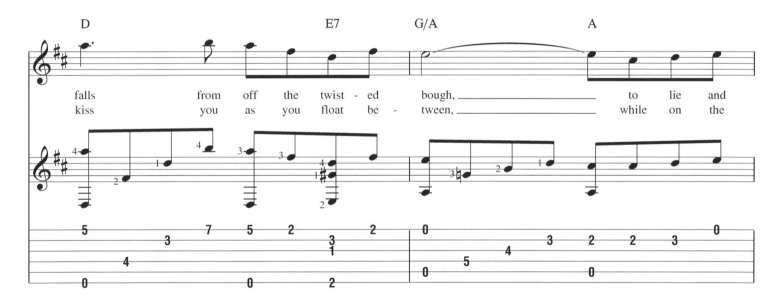

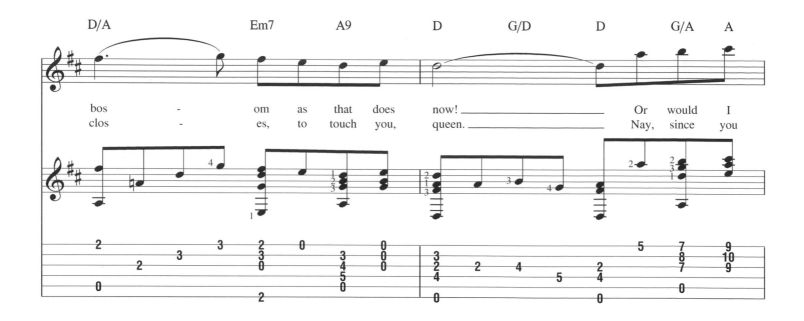

bos - - om as that does now! _____ Or would I
clos - - es, to touch you, queen. _____ Nay, since you

were a lit - tle bur - nish'd ap - ple _____ for you to
will not love, would I were grow - ing _____ a hap - py

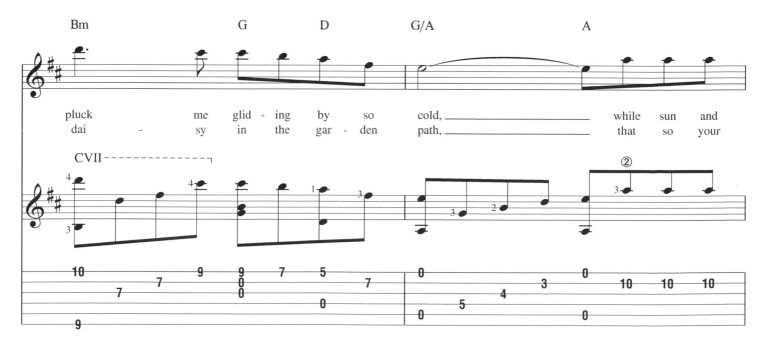

pluck me glid - ing by so cold, _____ while sun and
dai - sy in the gar - den path, _____ that so your

Molly Malone
(Cockles & Mussels)
Irish Folksong

Verse
Moderately

1. In Dub - lin's fair cit - y, where girls are ___ so
2., 3. *See additional lyrics*

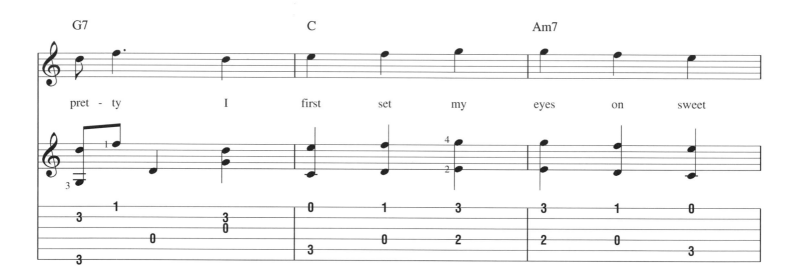

pret - ty   I   first   set   my   eyes   on   sweet

Mol - ly ___ Ma - lone.   As   she   pushed   her   wheel -

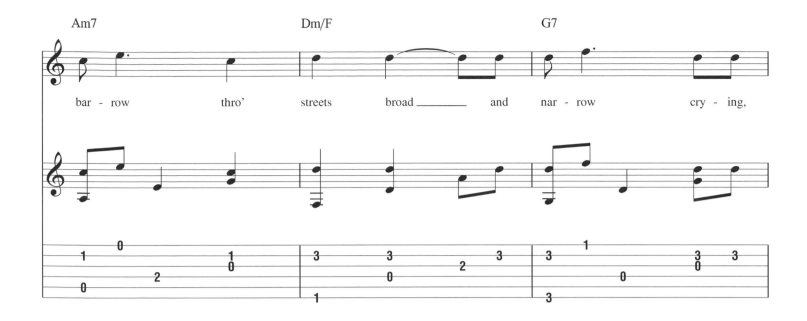

bar - row   thro'   streets   broad _____ and   nar - row   cry - ing,

"Cock - les ____ and   mus - sels,   a -   live,   a - live,

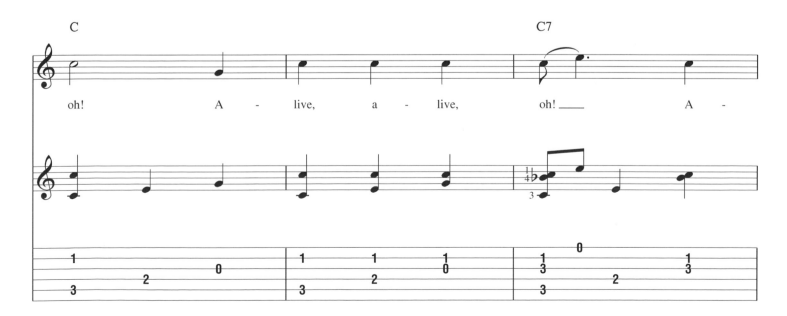

oh!   A -   live,   a -   live,   oh! ____   A -

Additional Lyrics

2. She was a fishmonger and sure 'twas no wonder,
   For so were her father and mother before.
   And they both wheeled their barrows through streets broad and narrow
   Crying, "Cockles and mussels, alive, alive, oh!

3. She died of a fever and no one could save her,
   And that was the end of sweet Molly Malone.
   Now her ghost wheels her barrow through streets broad and narrow
   Crying, "Cockles and mussels, alive, alive, oh!"

Star of County Down

Traditional Irish Folk Song

sheen of her nut - brown _ hair. Such a coax - ing elf, had to shake my - self to be

Chorus

sure I was real - ly there. Oh, from Ban - try Bay up to Der - ry Quay, and from

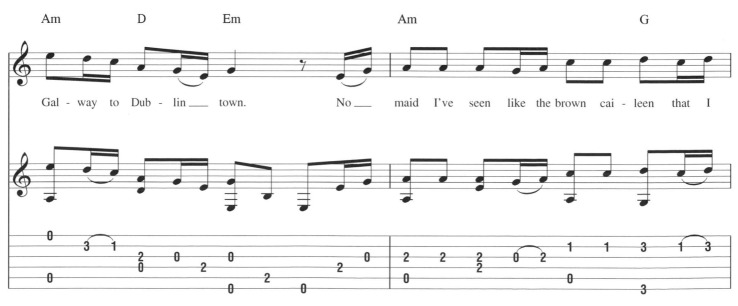

Gal - way to Dub - lin _ town. No _ maid I've seen like the brown cai - leen that I

Additional Lyrics

2. As she onward sped, I shook my head
   And I gazed with a feeling rare.
   And I said, says I, to a passerby,
   "Who's the maid with the nut-brown hair?"
   He smiled at me, and with pride says he,
   "That's the gem of Ireland's crown.
   She's young Rosie McCann from the banks of the Bann;
   She's the star of the County Down."

3. At the harvest fair I'll surely be there
   And I'll dress in my Sunday clothes.
   And I'll try sheep's eyes, and delud' thrin lies
   On the heart of the nut-brown Rose.
   No pipe I'll smoke, no horse I'll yoke,
   Though with rust my plow turns brown.
   Till a smiling bride by my own fireside
   Sits the star of the County Down.

Water Is Wide

Traditional

Drop D tuning:
(low to high) D-A-D-G-B-E

Verse

Moderately

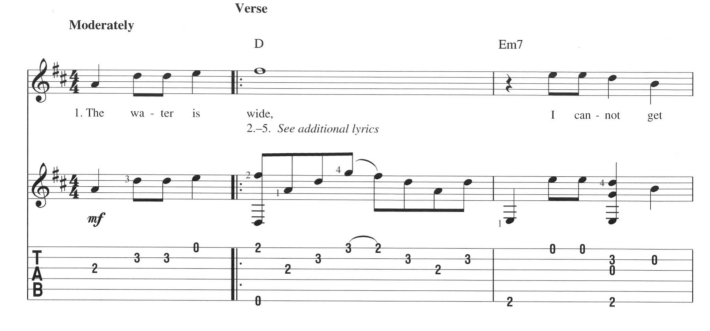

1. The wa - ter is wide,   I can - not get

2.–5. *See additional lyrics*

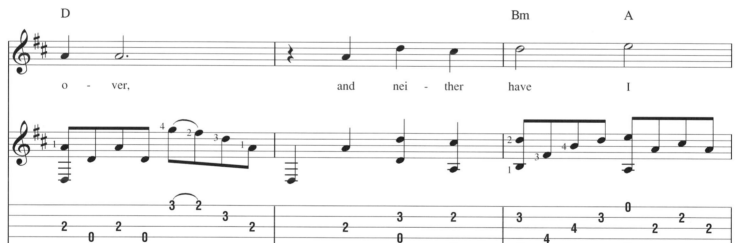

o - ver,   and nei - ther have I

wings to fly.   Give me a boat

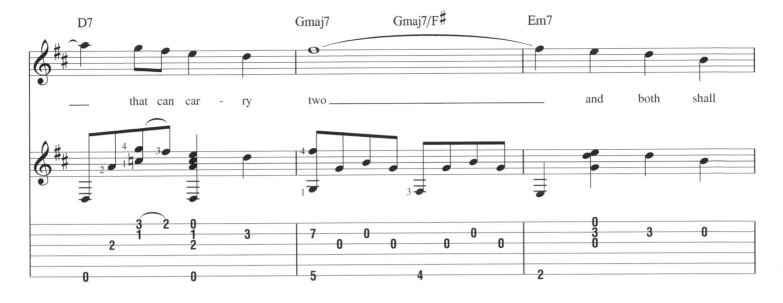

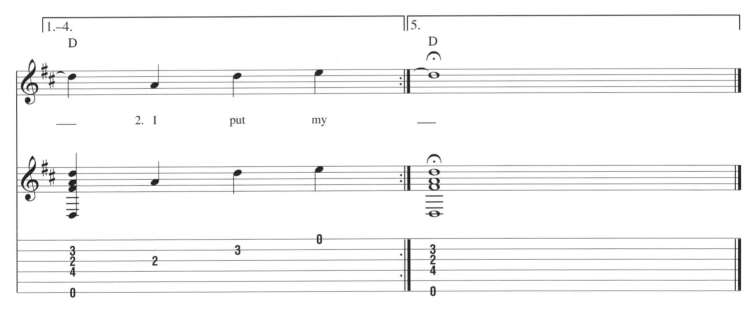

Additional Lyrics

2. I put my hand into some soft bush,
   Thinking the sweetest flower to find.
   The thorn it stuck me to the bone,
   And oh, I left that flower alone.

4. Oh, love is handsome and love is fine,
   Gay as a jewel when first it's new.
   But love grows old and waxes cold,
   And fades away like summer dew.

3. A ship there is and she sails the sea.
   She's loaded deep as deep can be.
   But not so deep as the love I'm in,
   And I know not how to sink or swim.

5. I leaned my back against a young oak,
   Thinking he was a trusty tree.
   But first he bended and then he broke,
   And thus did my false love to me.

The Wearing of the Green

Eighteenth Century Irish Folksong

1. Oh ___ Pad - dy dear, and did you hear the news that's go - ing
2., 3. *See additional lyrics*

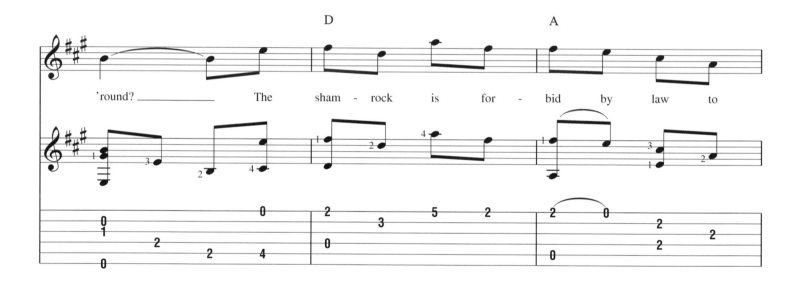

'round? ___ The sham - rock is for - bid by law to

grow on I - rish ground. Saint ___ Pat - rick's Day no

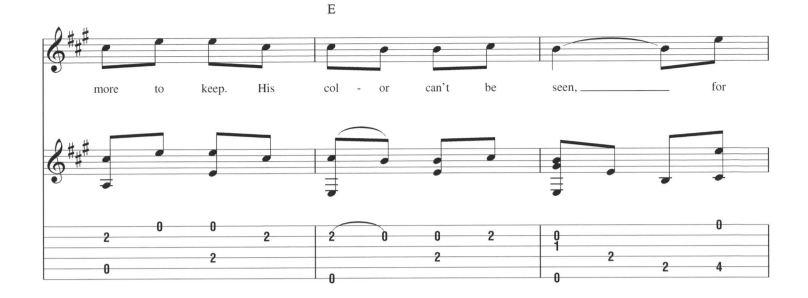

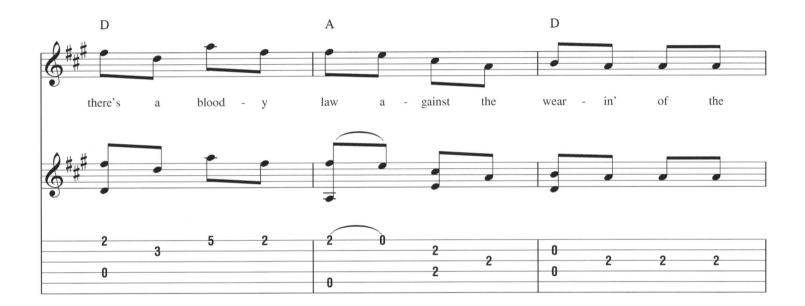

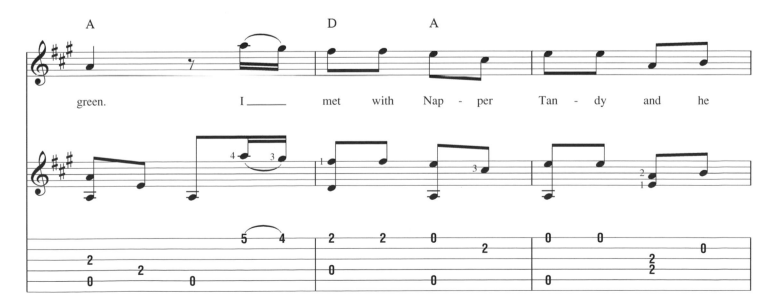

took me by the hand, and he said, "How's poor old

Ire - land and how _____ does she stand? She's the

most dis - tress - ful coun - try _____ that ev - er you have

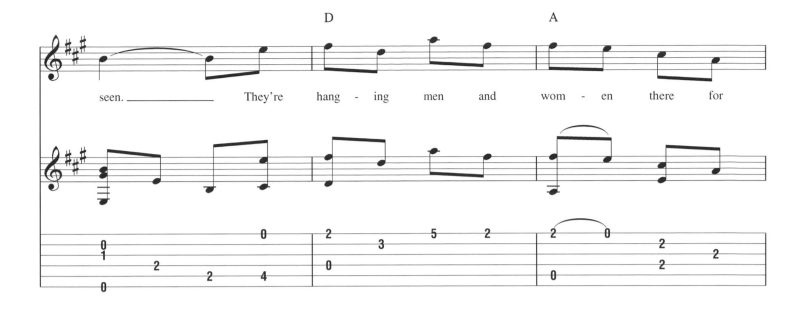

seen. _____ They're hang - ing men and wom - en there for

wear - ing of the green." 2. Then ___ green!

Additional Lyrics

2. Then since the color we must wear is England's cruel red,
   Ould Ireland's sons will ne'er forget the blood that they have shed.
   Then take the Shamrock from your hat and cast it to the sod;
   It will take root and flourish still, tho' under foot 'tis trod.
   When the law can stop the blades of grass from growing as they grow,
   And when the leaves in summer time their verdure dare not show,
   Then I will change the color I wear in my caubeen.
   But 'til that day, please God, I'll stick to wearing of the green!

3. But if, at last, her colors should be torn from Ireland's heart,
   Her sons, with shame and sorrow, from the dear old soil will part.
   I've heard whispers of a country that lies far beyond the sea
   Where rich and poor stand equal in the light of freedom's day!
   Oh Erin, must we leave you driven by the tyrant' hand?
   Must we ask a mother's blessing in a strange but happy land
   Where the cruel cross of England's thraldom never to be seen?
   But where, thank God, we'll live and die still wearing of the green!

When Irish Eyes Are Smiling

Words by Chauncey Olcott and George Graff, Jr.
Music by Ernest R. Ball

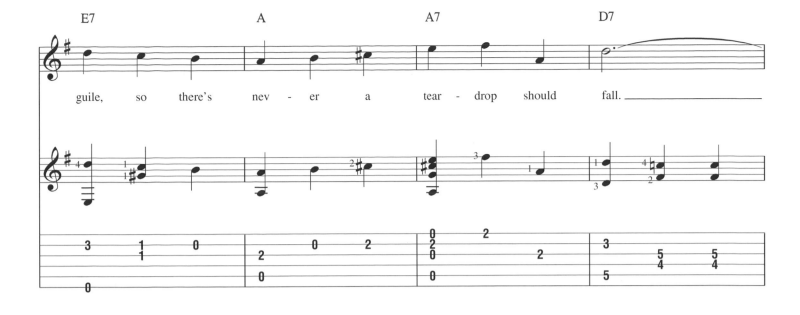

guile, so there's nev - er a tear - drop should fall. _____

_____ When your sweet lilt - ing laugh - ter's like some fair - y

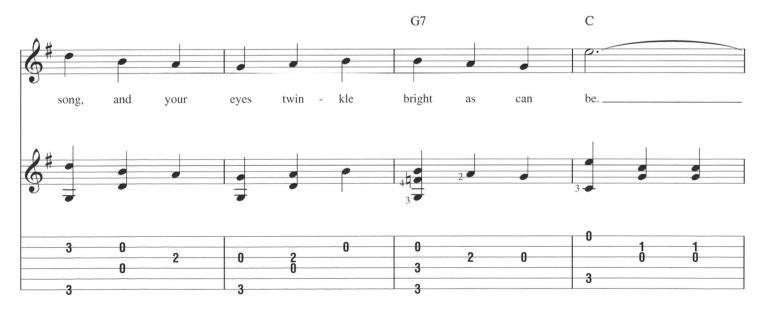

song, and your eyes twin - kle bright as can be. _____

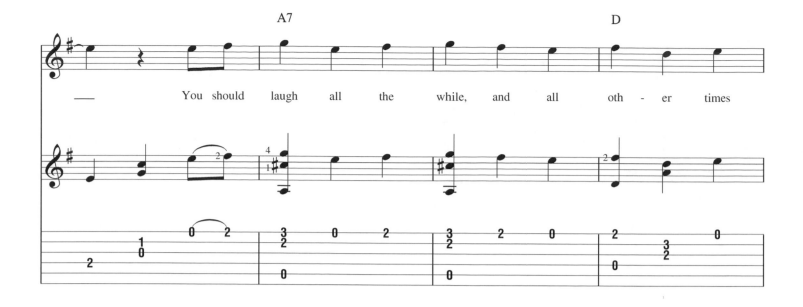

You should laugh all the while, and all oth - er times

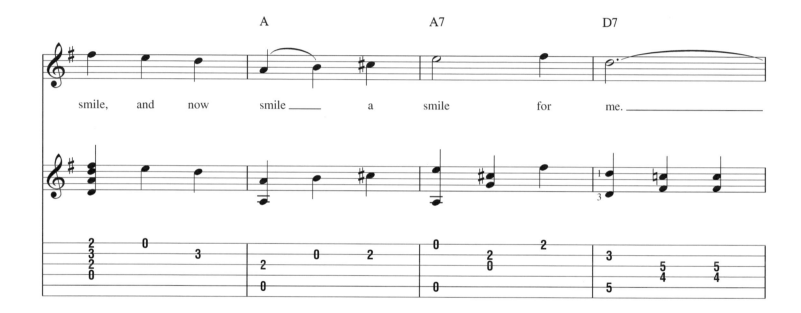

smile, and now smile _____ a smile for me. _____

Chorus

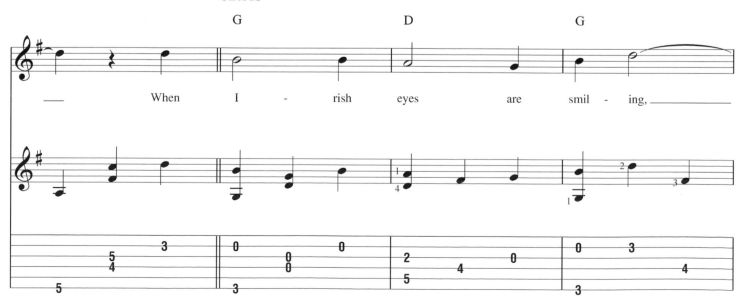

When I - rish eyes are smil - ing, _____

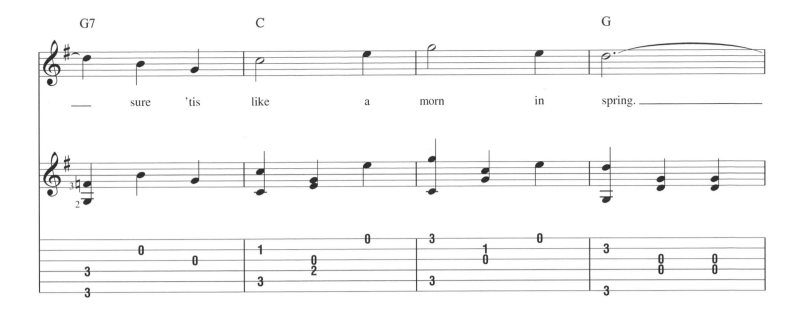

sure 'tis like a morn in spring. _____ _____

_____ In the lilt of I - rish laugh - ter,

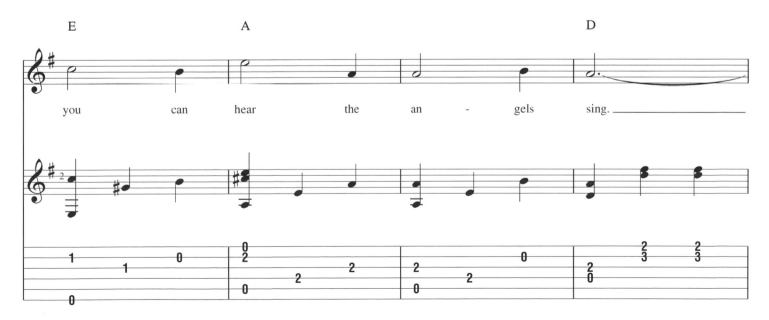

you can hear the an - gels sing. _____

When I - rish hearts are hap - py, _____

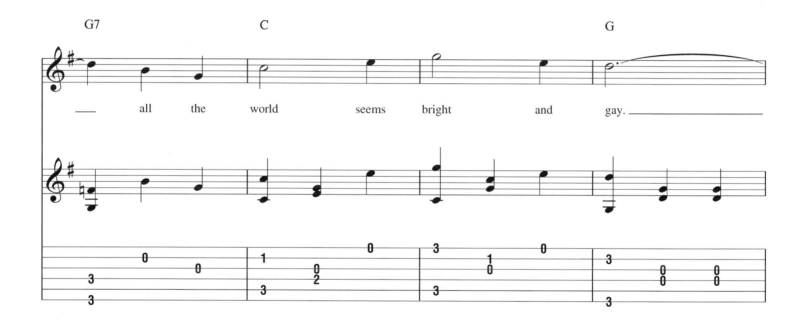

___ all the world seems bright and gay. _____

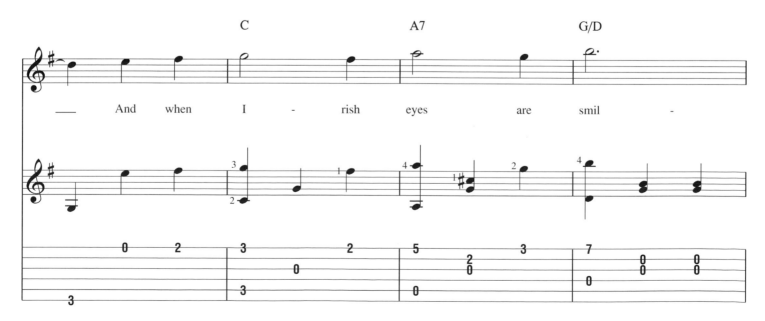

___ And when I - rish eyes are smil -

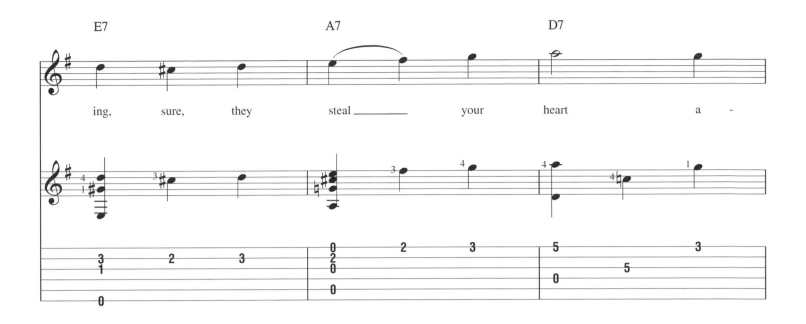

ing,   sure,   they   steal _____ your   heart   a -

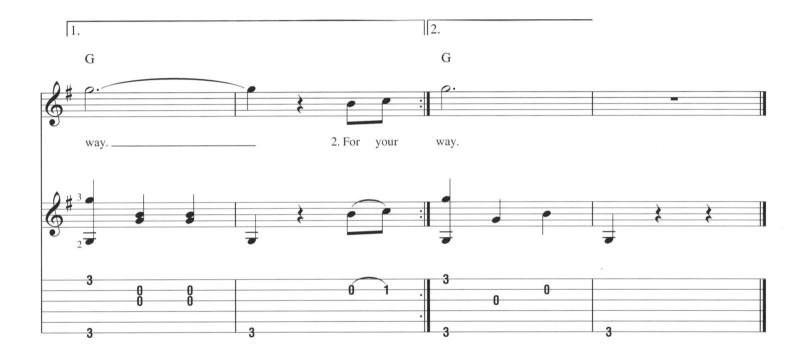

way. _____   2. For   your   way.

Additional Lyrics

2. For your smile is a part of the love in your heart,
   And it makes even sunshine more bright.
   Like the linnet's sweet song, crooning all the day long,
   Comes your laughter so tender and light.
   For the springtime of life is the sweetest of all
   There is ne'er a real care or regret;
   And while springtime is ours throughout all of youth's hours,
   Let us smile each chance we get.

Whiskey in the Jar

Traditional Irish Folk Song

Verse
Moderately

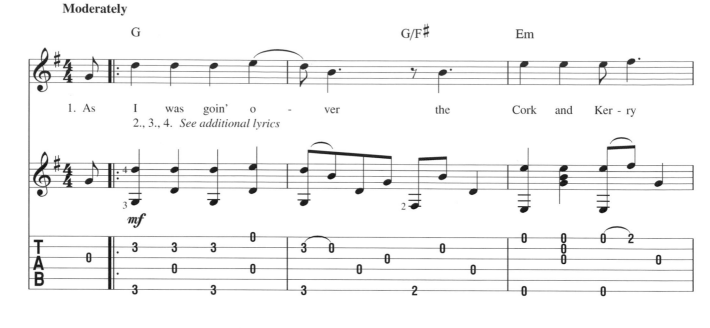

1. As I was goin' o - ver the Cork and Ker - ry
2., 3., 4. *See additional lyrics*

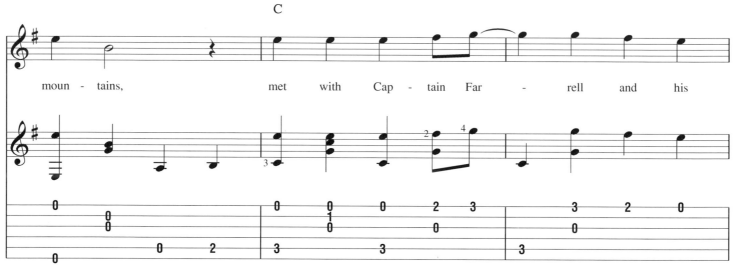

moun - tains, met with Cap - tain Far - rell and his

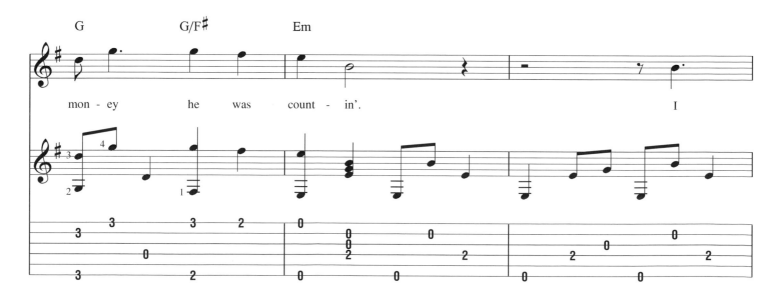

mon - ey he was count - in'. I

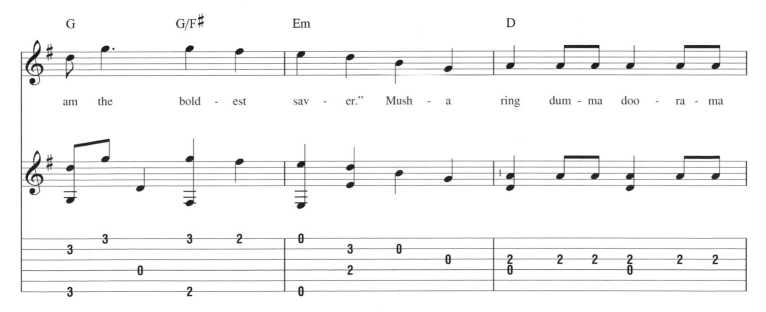

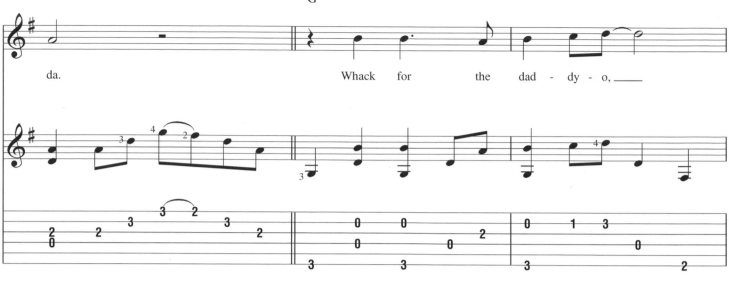

da.   Whack   for   the   dad - dy - o, _____

whack   for   the   dad - dy - o. _____   There's   whis - key   in   the

|1., 2., 3.| |4.|

jar.   2. I   jar.   Mush - a
                                    3. It was
                                    4. Some

Outro-Chorus

ring dum-ma doo - ra - ma da.   Whack for the dad - dy - o, ___

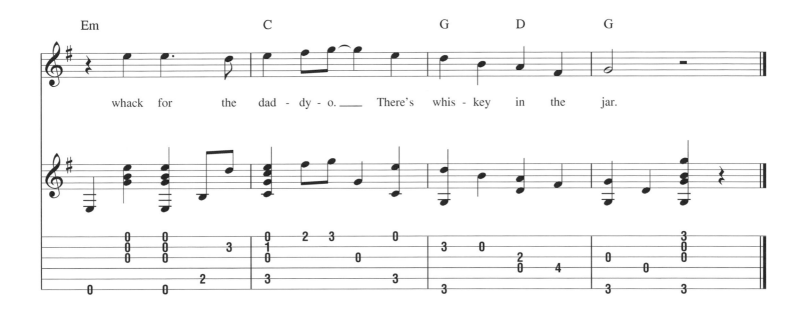

whack for the dad - dy - o. ___ There's whis - key in the jar.

Additional Lyrics

2. I counted out his money, and it made a pretty penny.
   I put it in my pocket and I took it home to Jenny.
   She said and she swore that she never would deceive me,
   But the devil take the women, for they never can be easy.
   With shareem dumma doo-rama da.

3. It was early in the morning as I rose up for travel,
   The guards were all around me and likewise Captain Farrell.
   I first produced my pistol, for she stole away my rapier,
   But I couldn't shoot the water, so a prisoner I was taken.
   Musha ring dumma doo-rama da.

4. Some take delight in the fishin' and the fowlin';
   Others take delight in the carriage gently rollin'.
   Ah, but I take delight in the juice of the barley,
   Courtin' pretty women in the mountains of Killarney.
   Musha ring dumma doo-rama da.

Wild Rover

Traditional Irish Folk Song

Verse

Moderately

1. I've been a wild ro - ver for man - y a
2., 3., 4. *See additional lyrics*

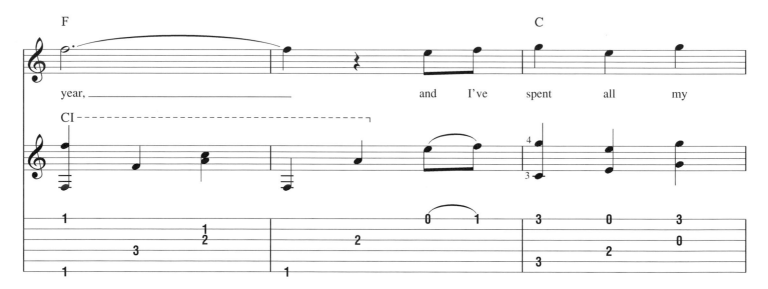

year, and I've spent all my

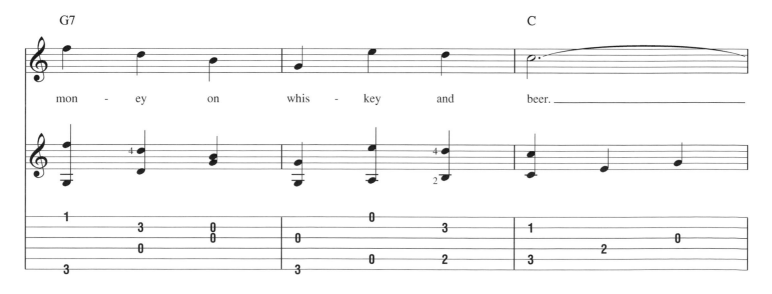

mon - ey on whis - key and beer.

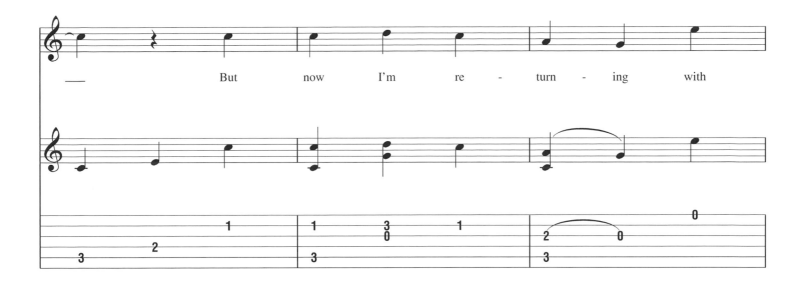

But now I'm re - turn - ing with

gold in great store, _____ and I nev - er will

play the wild ro - ver no more. And it's

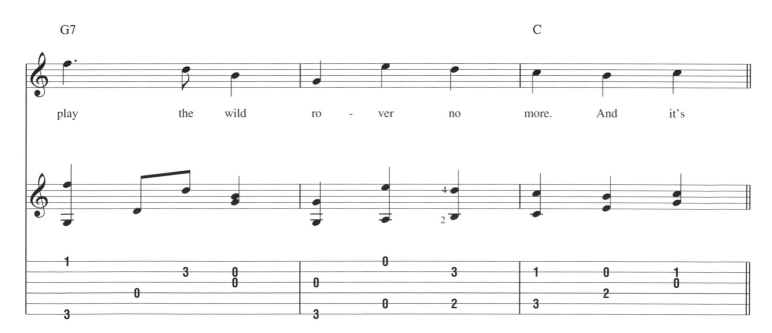

Chorus

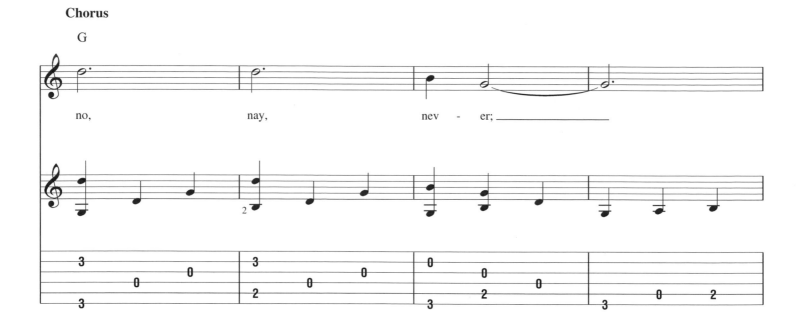

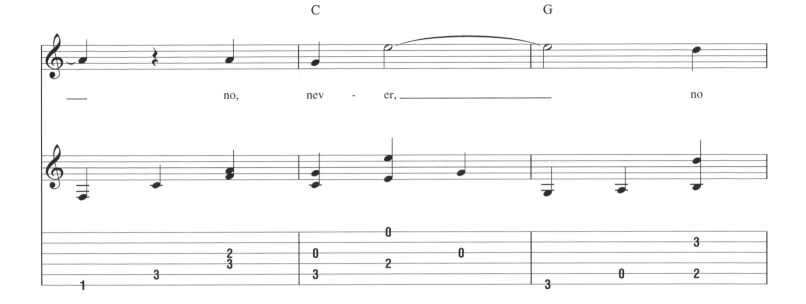

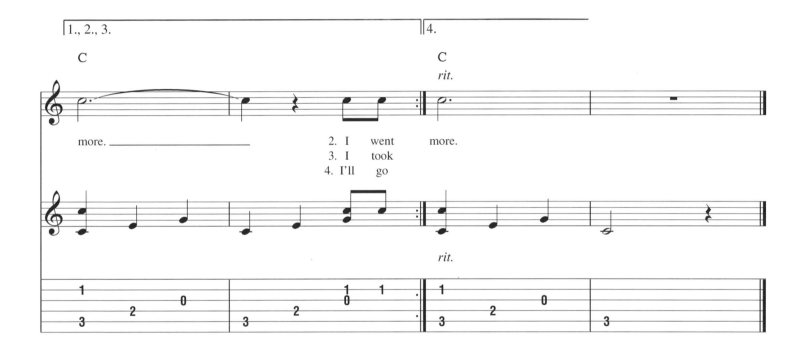

Additional Lyrics

2. I went into an alehouse I used to frequent
   And I told the landlady me money was spent.
   I asked her for credit, she answered me, "Nay,
   Such a custom as yours I can get any day."

3. I took up from my pocket ten sovereigns bright,
   And the landlady's eyes opened wide with delight.
   She says, "I have whiskeys and wines of the best,
   And the words that I said, sure, were only in jest."

4. I'll go home to my parents, confess what I've done,
   And I'll ask them to pardon their prodigal son.
   And if they caress me as oft times before,
   Sure I never will play the wild rover no more.

Sweet Rosie O'Grady

Words and Music by Maude Nugent

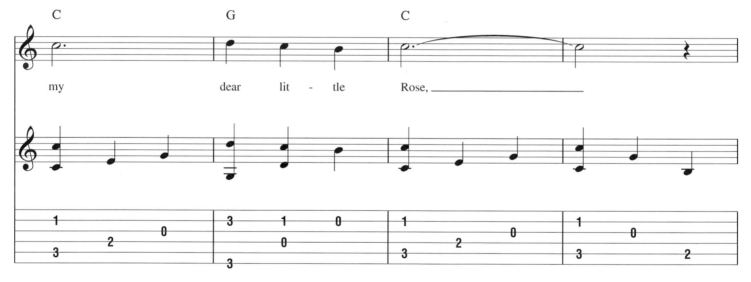

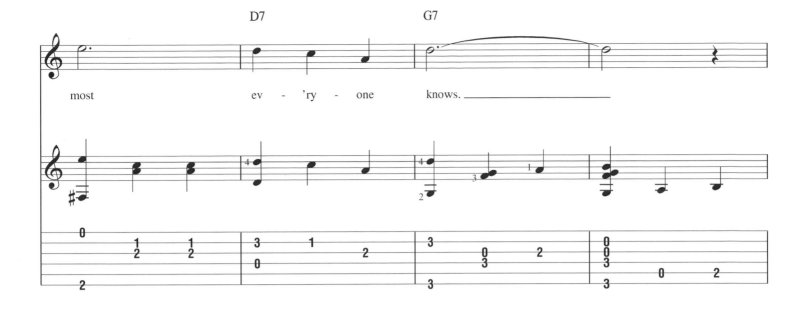

most   ev - 'ry - one   knows. _____

And   when   we   are   mar -   ried,

how   hap - py we'll   be. _____

I love sweet Ro - sie O' - Gra - dy and

Ro - sie O' - Gra - dy loves me.

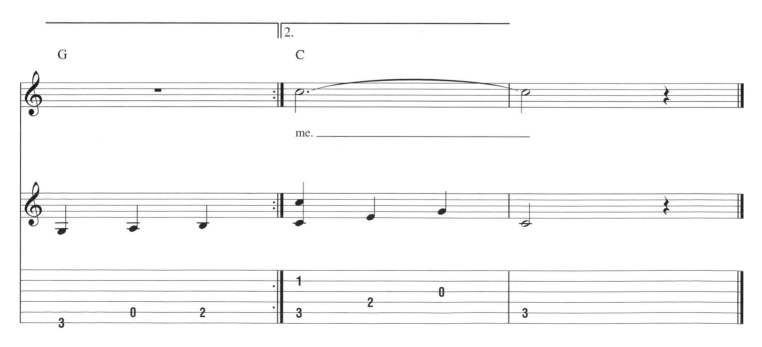

me.